SPOTLIGHT ON
IMMIGRATION AND MIGRATION

BROKEN TREATIES

NATIVE AMERICAN MIGRATIONS

Richard Alexander

PowerKiDS
press™

NEW YORK

Published in 2016 by The Rosen Publishing Group, Inc.
29 East 21st Street, New York, NY 10010

Editor: Katie Kawa
Book Design: Katelyn E. Reynolds

Photo Credits: Cover, p. 14 MPI/Getty Images; p. 5 AFP/Getty Images; pp. 6, 7 George Catlin/ Smithsonian American Art Museum; p. 9 Stock Montage/Getty Images; p. 11 Tungsten/Wikimedia Commons; p. 13 (map) Nikater/Wikimedia Commons; p. 13 (Andrew Jackson) File Upload Bot (Magnus Manske)/Wikimedia Commons; p. 15 Woolarac Museum, Bartlesville, Oklahoma; p. 17 SuperStock/Getty Images; p. 19 (Armstrong and Sitting Bull) Library of Congress/ Wikimedia Commons; p. 19 (bottom) DeAgostini/Getty Images; p. 21 Courtesy of the Library of Congress; p. 22 David W. Hamilton/The Image Bank/Getty Images.

Library of Congress Cataloging-in-Publication Data

Alexander, Richard, author.
 Broken treaties : Native American migrations / Richard Alexander.
    pages cm. — (Spotlight on immigration and migration)
 Includes index.
 ISBN 978-1-5081-4056-6 (pbk.)
 ISBN 978-1-5081-4057-3 (6 pack)
 ISBN 978-1-5081-4059-7 (library binding)
 1. Indian Removal, 1813-1903—Juvenile literature. 2. Indians of North America—Migrations—Juvenile literature. I. Title.
 E98.R4A44 2016
 323.1197—dc23
                              2015021407

Manufactured in the United States of America

CPSIA Compliance Information: Batch #BW16PK: For further information contact Rosen Publishing, New York, New York at 1-800-237-9932.

CONTENTS

FROM ASIA TO AMERICA

The **ancestors** of Native Americans were the first people to settle in the Western Hemisphere, but even they came from somewhere else. In fact, they were the first **immigrants** to call the Americas home. Historians believe the ancestors of Native Americans **emigrated** from Asia around 15,000 to 25,000 years ago, but they could have arrived even earlier than that. Historians believe they crossed the Bering Land Bridge from Asia into North America. Then, they settled all over both North America and South America.

By the time the Europeans started to colonize North America and South America in the 1500s, millions of Native Americans were living there. Many of those Native Americans were forced to migrate from their homelands to other parts of the Americas as European colonies continued to grow.

When Christopher Columbus landed in the Americas in 1492, he believed he'd found the East Indies. He called the people he saw *Indios*, which is the Spanish word for "Indians."

DIFFERENT PLACES, DIFFERENT TRIBES

Long before Europeans began to arrive in the Americas, Native Americans formed settlements where they found good land for farming and hunting. Different tribes settled in different areas, and the lands around them determined their way of life.

This painting by George Catlin shows Sioux Indians using snowshoes and spears to hunt bison in winter.

The tribes that settled in the southeastern part of North America, such as the Cherokee and the Seminole, hunted, gathered wild fruits and vegetables, and farmed. The Native Americans of the Great Plains, such as the Sioux, followed the herds of bison they hunted. These people lived in tepees made of bison skins. The tribes that settled in the southwestern part of North America, including the Apaches and Pueblos, hunted and grew crops, such as corn, beans, and squash. These tribes adapted to life in the harsh desert regions of North America.

This painting by George Catlin shows a large Comanche village filled with their familiar tepees. In the right corner, women prepare bison skins for clothing. Dogs can be seen along the left side. The horses became part of Comanche life after Europeans brought the animals to the Americas.

THE EUROPEANS ARRIVE

As the British began to emigrate to the eastern part of North America in the early 1600s, they encountered various Native American tribes already living in those areas. From the beginning, relations between the British immigrants and the Native Americans were strained. Many conflicts broke out between those two groups of people.

The British colonists and the Native Americans had very different ideas about land ownership. The Native Americans didn't think that land could be owned by one person. The colonists, however, wanted to own the land. Many colonists didn't want to share it with the Native Americans. The Native Americans were angry that the colonists settled wherever they liked without caring if other people already lived there. These **tensions** grew as more colonists continued to immigrate from Europe.

The Pequot War was fought from 1636 to 1637 between members of the Pequot tribe and colonists in areas that would become Massachusetts and Connecticut, as well as their Native American **allies**.

EXPANDING AMERICA

With the signing of the Declaration of Independence in 1776, the 13 British colonies in North America became the independent United States. The new nation then began to **expand**. In 1803, President Thomas Jefferson more than doubled the size of the United States through the Louisiana Purchase, in which he bought the western Louisiana Territory from France.

Jefferson then named Meriwether Lewis and William Clark as leaders of an expedition to explore this new land and find a passage that connected the Atlantic Ocean to the Pacific Ocean. They left in May 1804. On their travels, Lewis and Clark encountered many Native Americans, who were told their lands now belonged to the United States. Westward expansion meant new challenges for the relationship between settlers and Native Americans.

Lewis and Clark met many friendly Native Americans during their expedition. Sacagawea was a member of the Shoshone tribe who helped guide Lewis and Clark during their expedition through the new western lands of the United States.

MOVING WESTWARD

The Louisiana Purchase gave Americans the opportunity to move westward. However, most Americans didn't want to leave their homes in the eastern part of the country. They wanted to remove the Native Americans from those eastern lands, and the U.S. government agreed.

In 1830, President Andrew Jackson signed the Indian Removal Act into law. This law stated Native American nations would be given unsettled lands west of the Mississippi River in exchange for their eastern lands. Many Native American nations agreed to sign over their lands and settle peacefully in the West. However, southeastern nations, such as the Cherokee, the Seminole, and the Creek, refused to leave their homelands. They didn't want to migrate to new lands after living in the southeast for hundreds of years.

Members of the Cherokee nation refused to leave their homelands after the Indian Removal Act was passed. However, the U.S. government ultimately forced members of the Cherokee nation and other tribes to migrate westward from their homelands, as shown on this map.

Andrew Jackson

13

THE TRAIL OF TEARS

If Native Americans didn't agree to move west, the Indian Removal Act allowed the U.S. government to force them to leave their homelands. The Cherokee nation was one Native American group that was forcibly removed from their eastern homelands. They refused to move west, so the U.S. government sent soldiers to their lands in 1838 to make them leave.

This illustration shows U.S. soldiers attacking Native Americans, which often happened when Native Americans refused to leave their homelands.

Thousands of Cherokee people were forced to march west. The journey from their homelands to Indian Territory in what is now Oklahoma was long and dangerous. Deadly **diseases** killed many Cherokees along the way, and others died from **starvation** on the journey. Historians believe at least 4,000 Cherokees died during this forced migration, which became known as the Trail of Tears.

Members of the Cherokee nation were forced to travel over land and water in order to reach Indian Territory. Some historians believe they traveled over 1,000 miles (1,609 km) on the journey.

NEW WESTERN SETTLERS

More Americans began moving west by the 1840s. This was particularly true during the California gold rush, which began in 1848. Western settlers used routes such as the Oregon Trail, the Mormon Trail, and the Santa Fe Trail. The building of the Union Pacific and the Central Pacific Railroads in the 1860s allowed even greater numbers of people to travel west.

As westward expansion continued and the number of immigrants coming to America started to rise, people needed more land. This meant more trouble for Native Americans, who once again were living on land settlers now wanted. This time, many Native American nations wouldn't give up their lands without a fight. They used force to **protect** their homelands against settlers who claimed the land was theirs.

Native Americans in the West fought back against settlers trying to take their lands by attacking wagon trains on westward trails.

CUSTER'S LAST STAND

When gold was discovered on lands the U.S. government gave to the Cheyenne and the Lakota Sioux tribes, tensions began to rise between white settlers and the Native Americans living there. The settlers wanted to mine for gold on those lands, but the Native Americans fought back.

In 1876, U.S. troops led by George Armstrong Custer were sent to force the Cheyenne and the Lakota Sioux people onto their reservation, or the piece of land set aside for them by the U.S. government. However, the Native Americans, led by Sitting Bull, fought against the U.S. soldiers in what's now Montana during what became known as the Battle of the Little Bighorn. All Custer's troops were killed in the battle, which became known as Custer's Last Stand. It was the most **decisive** victory for the Native Americans against white settlers on the Great Plains.

George Armstrong Custer

Sitting Bull

The Battle of the Little Bighorn was one of the last major efforts by Native Americans to **violently** fight back against forced migration.

19

WOUNDED KNEE

The Battle of the Little Bighorn was far from the last armed conflict between Native Americans and white settlers. Even though Native Americans celebrated some victories, they ultimately lost many people and all their land. As the U.S. government took more and more land for the growing country, it set aside areas of land for reservations for Native Americans to live on.

By the end of the 1800s, after much bloodshed and loss, most Native Americans had been moved to reservations in the West. In 1890, a **massacre** occurred at Wounded Knee in present-day South Dakota. Many Native Americans were killed, and the loss marked the end of Native American efforts to fight back against the U.S. government.

The tensions that led to the massacre at Wounded Knee, which is sometimes called the Battle of Wounded Knee, started to rise when Sitting Bull was killed by reservation police. Shown here is a reenactment of the massacre from 1913.

LIFE ON THE RESERVATION

About 5.2 million people of Native American **descent** are living in the United States today. Many of those people live on reservations. There are about 326 areas of land set aside by the U.S. government as Indian reservations. The largest is the Navajo Nation reservation, which includes parts of Arizona, New Mexico, and Utah. It covers over 17 million acres (6.9 million ha) of land.

Although Native Americans were often forced to migrate far from their homelands, they still kept their **traditional** way of life alive in new places. This helped them during difficult times. Today, those traditions help connect them to their history in a way that fills them with pride.

GLOSSARY

ally: One of two or more people or groups who work together.

ancestor: One of the people from whom a person is descended.

decisive: Very clear and obvious.

descent: The background of a person in terms of their family or nationality.

disease: A sickness.

emigrate: To leave a country or region to live somewhere else.

expand: To become bigger.

immigrant: A person who comes to a country to live there.

massacre: The violent killing of many people.

protect: To keep safe.

starvation: Suffering or death caused by having nothing or not enough to eat.

tension: A state in which two people, groups, or countries disagree with and feel anger toward each other.

traditional: Having to do with the ways of doing things in a culture that are passed down from parents to children.

violently: Done by using physical force in a way meant to cause harm to someone.

INDEX

PRIMARY SOURCE LIST

p. 6
Sioux Indians on Snowshoes Lancing Buffalo. Created by George Catlin. 1846–1848. Oil on canvas. Now kept at the Smithsonian American Art Museum, Washington, D.C.

p. 7
Comanche Village, Women Dressing Robes and Drying Meat. Created by George Catlin. 1834–1835. Oil on canvas. Now kept at the Smithsonian American Art Museum, Washington, D.C.

p. 19
General George Armstrong Custer. Creator unknown. May 23, 1865. Photograph. Now kept at the Library of Congress Prints and Photographs Division, Washington, D.C.

p. 19
Sitting Bull. Created by David Francis Barry. ca. 1885. Photograph. Now kept at the Library of Congress Prints and Photographs Division, Washington, D.C.

WEBSITES

Due to the changing nature of Internet links, PowerKids Press has developed an online list of websites related to the subject of this book. This site is updated regularly. Please use this link to access the list: www.powerkidslinks.com/soim/brtr